my itty-bitty bio

Judy Heumann

T0002045

easterseals

CHERRY LAKE PRESS

Published in the United States of America by Cherry Lake Publishing Group
Ann Arbor, Michigan
www.cherrylakepublishing.com

Reading Adviser: Beth Walker Gambro, MS, Ed., Reading Consultant, Yorkville, IL
Book Designer: Jennifer Wahi
Illustrator: Jeff Bane

Photo Credits: © Albert Pego/Shutterstock, 5; © alexeisido shutterstock/Shutterstock, 7; © Leonard Zhukovsky/Shutterstock, 9; © LCV/Shutterstock, 11; © Ajay Suresh via Wikimedia Commons (BY CC 2.0), 13; © Kirill Shashkov/Shutterstock, 15; © Gorodenkoff/Shutterstock, 17, 22; Taylordw, CC BY-SA 4.0, via Wikimedia Commons, 19; East Asia and Pacific Media Hub U.S. Department of State, Public domain, via Wikimedia Commons, 21, 23

Cherry Lake Press is an imprint of Cherry Lake Publishing Group.

Library of Congress Cataloging-in-Publication Data

Names: Newton, Lily (Author of children's books), author. | Bane, Jeff, 1957- illustrator.
Title: Judy Heumann / written by Lily Newton ; illustrated by Jeff Bane.
Description: Ann Arbor, Michigan : Cherry Lake Publishing, [2023] | Series: My itty-bitty bio | Audience: Grades K-1 | Summary: "Judy Heumann, a leader in the disabled community, has made the world more accessible. This biography for early readers examines her life in a simple, age-appropriate way that helps young readers develop word recognition and reading skills. Developed in partnership with Easterseals and written by a member of the disability community, this title helps all readers learn from those who make a difference in our world. The My Itty-Bitty Bio series celebrates diversity, inclusion, and the values that readers of all ages can aspire to"-- Provided by publisher.
Identifiers: LCCN 2023009132 | ISBN 9781668927250 (hardcover) | ISBN 9781668928301 (paperback) | ISBN 9781668929773 (ebook) | ISBN 9781668931257 (pdf)
Subjects: LCSH: Heumann, Judy E. | People with disabilities--United States--Biography--Juvenile literature. | Human rights workers--United States--Biography--Juvenile literature. | Teachers--United States--Biography--Juvenile literature.
Classification: LCC HV3013.H48 N49 2023 | DDC 362.4--dc23/eng/20230224
LC record available at https://lccn.loc.gov/2023009132

Printed in the United States of America
Corporate Graphics

Note from the author on Judy Heumann's passing in March, 2023.
Judy Heumann was the mother of the disability rights movement. Us disabled folk are forever grateful for the work she did to fight for our rights. To fight all injustice is to continue Judy's legacy. Be proud of who you are and try to make the world a better place. That's what Judy would want.

About the author: Lily Newton is a writer, filmmaker, and content creator. After a lifetime of feeling different, she finally got to understand herself in her early 20's when she found out she is autistic. Ever since then, disability advocacy has been a driving force in her life. When not working on creative work, Lily spends her free time doing yoga and snuggling with her adorable cat.

About the illustrator: Jeff Bane and his two business partners own a studio along the American River in Folsom, California, home of the 1849 Gold Rush. When Jeff's not sketching or illustrating for clients, he's either swimming or kayaking in the river to relax.

About our partnership: This title was developed in partnership with Easterseals to support its mission of empowering people with disabilities. Through their national network of affiliates, Easterseals provides essential services and on-the-ground supports to more than 1.5 million people each year.

I was born in Brooklyn, New York. My parents were Jewish **immigrants**.

Where were you born?

I got sick. I could no longer walk.
I used a wheelchair.

I could not go to many schools.
The schools were not **accessible**.

My mom found a school for me. I was 9 years old. I rode the bus with my wheelchair.

How do you get to school?

I went to college. I wanted to be a teacher. I took all the classes.

People said I could not teach. This was not fair. It was because I was disabled.

I filed a **lawsuit**. I worked with **civil rights** lawyers. My case went to a court.

I wanted to help people like me.
I became an **advocate**.

I passed away in 2023. My legacy lives on. I wrote books. I worked to pass laws. I worked to create **justice**.

What would you like to ask me?

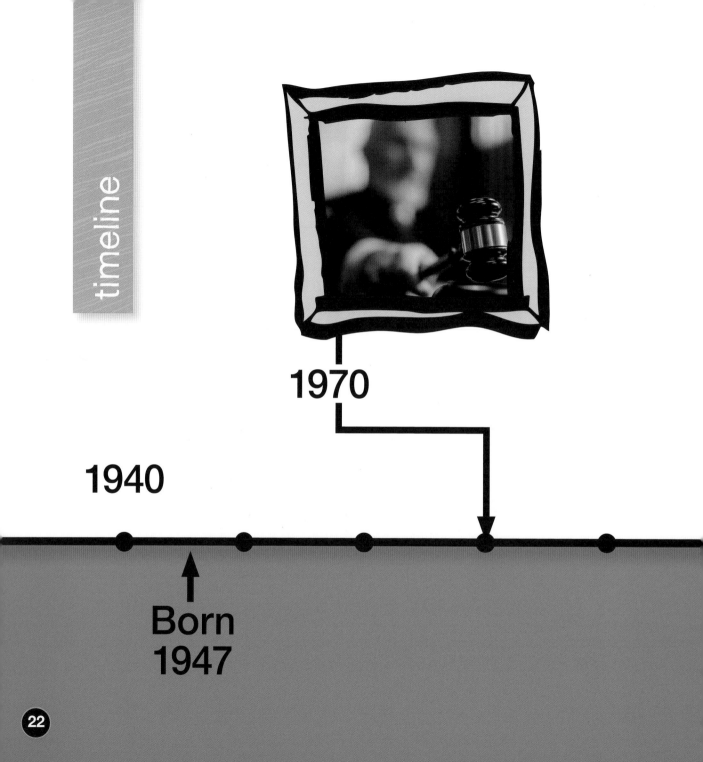

1970

1940

Born
1947

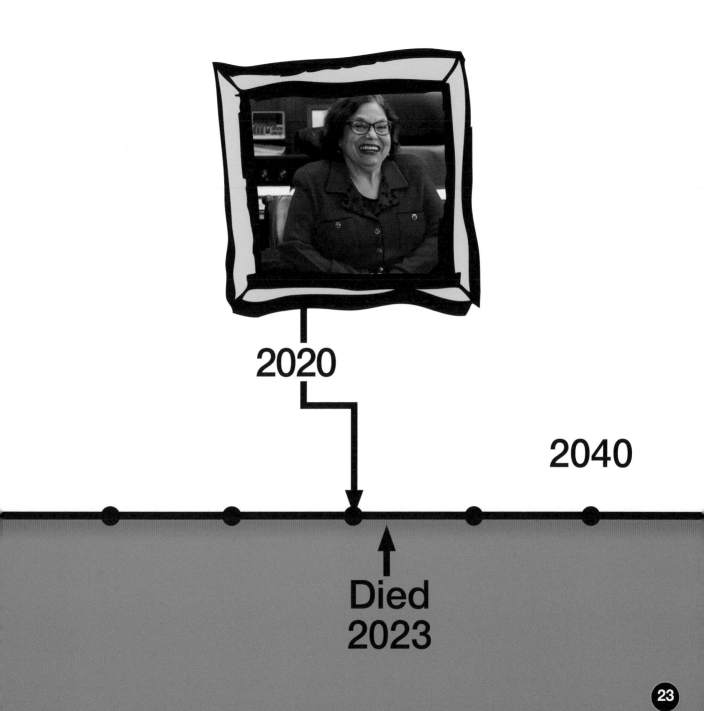

2020

2040

Died
2023

glossary

accessible (ack-SESS-uh-ble) able to be accessed or used by everyone

advocate (AD-vuh-kuht) a person who defends the rights of others

immigrants (IM-meh-grints) people who move to live in a different country

justice (JUS-tuhs) fairness

lawsuit (LAW-soot) a request for a fair decision based on the law from a court or judge

index